TRAVELLING WILD

SAILING
THE GREAT BARRIER REEF

WAYLAND
www.waylandbooks.co.uk

Published in paperback in 2014 by Wayland

Copyright © Wayland 2014

Wayland
Hachette Children's Books
338 Euston Road
London NW1 3BR

Wayland Australia
Level 17/207 Kent Street
Sydney NSW 2000

Commissioning editor: Debbie Foy
Designer: Lisa Peacock
Consultant: Michael Scott
Proofreader/indexer: Susie Brooks
Map illustrator: Tim Hutchinson

A catalogue for this title is available
from the British Library
919.4'3

ISBN: 978 0 7502 8325 0

Printed in China

10 9 8 7 6 5 4 3 2 1

Wayland is a division of Hachette Children's Books,
an Hachette UK Company.
www.hachette.co.uk

CONTENTS

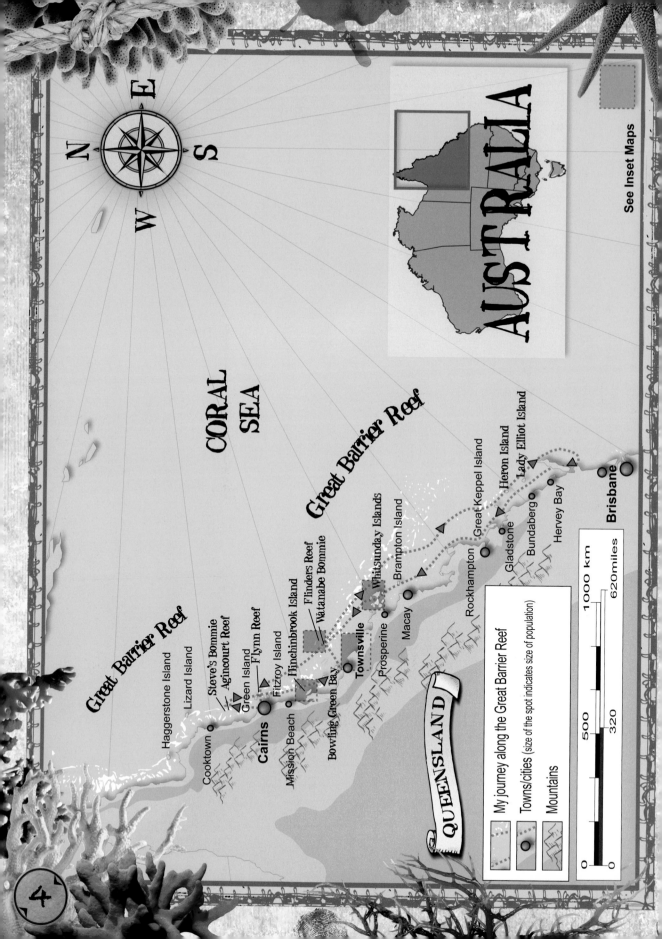

AUSTRALIA

See Inset Maps

CORAL SEA

Great Barrier Reef

Great Barrier Reef

Great Barrier Reef

Haggerstone Island

Lizard Island

Cooktown

Steve's Bommie
Agincourt Reef
Green Island
Flynn Reef

Cairns

Fitzroy Island

Mission Beach

Hinchinbrook Island

Flinders Reef
Watanabe Bommie

Bowling Green Bay

Townsville

Prosperine

Whitsunday Islands

Brampton Island

Macay

Rockhampton

Great Keppel Island

Gladstone

Heron Island

Bundaberg

Lady Elliot Island

Hervey Bay

Brisbane

QUEENSLAND

My journey along the Great Barrier Reef

Towns/cities (size of the spot indicates size of population)

Mountains

1000 km

500

620miles

320

4

THE WORLD'S BIGGEST CORAL REEF

Preparing for the trip

I'm so excited! For the next five months I'll be sailing and diving the Great Barrier Reef. I have visions of undersea coral gardens, shoals of tropical fish and giant turtles swimming by. I know there will be dangers — crocodiles, sharks and poisonous jellyfish — but I hope, if I follow the safety advice, I'll stay safe. I've been training for weeks, and I'm about as ready as I'll ever be. Now I just want to be on my boat with the sea breeze in my face.

Rainforest of the sea

A coral reef is an underwater structure made of a hard substance called calcium carbonate, which is produced by tiny animals called coral polyps. Coral reefs are found mainly in warm, shallow seas. They're often called the rainforests of the sea because of the extraordinary diversity of species found living on them.

A living system

The Great Barrier Reef is the world's largest coral reef and one of the seven natural wonders of the world. Located in the Coral Sea off the coast of Queensland, Australia, it is composed of over 2,900 reefs and 900 islands, and stretches for more than 2,600 km. Bigger than the Great Wall of China, the Great Barrier Reef is the world's biggest single living structure and the only one visible from space. Much of the reef has been declared a marine park and is protected from human activities such as fishing and tourism.

Equipment

- waterproof clothing
- lifejacket
- deck shoes
- sailing gloves
- sun hat
- sunscreen
- seasickness medication
- wetsuit, mask, flippers, snorkel
- scuba gear
- diving knife
- dive light
- dive computer
- weight belt
- map and compass

A TOURISTS' PARADISE

5 September

I began my journey yesterday, setting sail from Cairns and heading north to Agincourt Reef. This is a ribbon reef – one of the long, thin strips of reef that mark the outer edges of the Great Barrier Reef. I did a 'shakedown dive' to get used to my new kit, my dive buddies and the crystal clear waters. I had great views of the amazing coral and marine life. I was amazed at how many tourists there were compared to my last visit five years ago. I saw every kind of pleasure boat from dinghies to superyachts, as well as snorkellers and divers, and even a giant tourist platform.

A growing industry

Tourists have been visiting the Great Barrier Reef since the 1890s, but tourism only became a major industry in the 1970s and 80s. Today, thanks to improved transport links and technology, it's the biggest commercial activity in the region, generating 4–5 billion Australian dollars every year. Boat tours are offered, from day trips to longer voyages, and the most popular tourist activities include scuba diving and snorkelling. Tourists can also hire fishing boats, glass–bottomed boats and semi–submersibles, indulge in water sports, or go on helicopter tours.

Environmental concerns

Environmental campaigners are concerned that all this tourist activity may be having a damaging effect on the reef system. Researchers have noted, for example, that coral is 15 times more likely to be diseased at sites with tourist platforms. This may be caused by seabirds, which land on the platforms. Their droppings contain chemicals that are toxic when washed into the sea. Other damage is caused by tourists standing on or bumping into corals while diving and snorkelling.

Around 90% of reef life occurs within 4 m of the surface, so snorkelling is often the best and easiest way to explore the Great Barrier Reef.

Be smart, survive!

Sunburn is a real danger here in the Coral Sea. I try to avoid being on deck during the middle part of the day. When I am on deck, I always wear a hat and use a high-factor (30+) sunscreen. I also make sure I drink plenty of water.

REEF FISH

15 September

I continued south to Flynn Reef near Cairns. Over the next few weeks, I tried out a few of the dive sites there, such as Tracy's Bommie, Gordon's Mooring, Tennis Court and the Coral Gardens. I explored undersea cliffs and overhangs and even tried a spot of night diving. The sheer variety of fish species I saw there was breathtaking!

Dangerous creatures

There are several deadly species to try to avoid on the Great Barrier Reef. These include the irukanji jellyfish (a small creature with a venomous sting that can hospitalise an adult), the blue-ringed octopus (the size of a golf ball but with a beak that can penetrate a wetsuit and poison that can kill an adult in minutes), and the cone shell (pretty to look at, but if stood on it will fire a dart into the victim, containing venom potent enough to kill).

Diversity of fish

There are between 1,500 and 2,000 species of fish on the Great Barrier Reef, and it's possible to find at least 200 species in just one hectare (roughly the area of a football pitch). Most of these fish belong to just a few family groups.

- **Angelfish** are known for their gorgeous colours and markings, ranging from thin stripes to multi-coloured speckled patterns. They have a curious nature and are found at all levels of the upper reef.

- **Butterfly fish** are a close relative of the angelfish, and look similar except for their longer, thinner noses. They feed on corals and when they find a partner it's a lifelong bond.

- **Clownfish** are typically bright orange with a white or pale blue band. They live among the tentacles of sea anemones, being immune to their poisonous stinging cells. The anemone provides them with protection from predators.

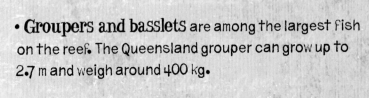

- **Damselfish** are small and timid and often gather in large schools above the reef, feeding on plankton.

- **Groupers and basslets** are among the largest fish on the reef. The Queensland grouper can grow up to 2.7 m and weigh around 400 kg.

- **Parrotfish** use their beak-like mouths to scrape algae from the coral, which they then eat. Parrotfish have the ability to change sex.

- **Surgeonfish** are among the most visually striking of reef fish, with their vivid blue and yellow markings. Their venomous fin spines protect them from predators.

WHALES AND DOLPHINS

28 September

Today as we began heading south from Flynn Reef, we had a great piece of luck! A dwarf minke whale approached and began circling the boat. I'd been hoping to see some whales before they returned south to Antarctica, but this was late in the year to see a minke. I grabbed my snorkelling gear and got into the water. At first, all I saw was blue water. Then a shape appeared. The young minke was about 3 m long, and so streamlined and graceful. I watched, stunned, as she glided past.

The great migration

The Great Barrier Reef provides a breeding ground for some 30 species of cetaceans (whales and dolphins). The most commonly seen near Cairns are dwarf minke whales, humpback whales and bottlenose dolphins. One regular visitor is the Migaloo ('white fella'), the all-white humpback, first spotted in 1991. He is the world's only documented white humpback. Around 4,000 humpbacks spend the southern summer in the Antarctic before migrating to the Great Barrier Reef between June and October to calve and build up their strength.

Humpback whales often leap out of the water. This is called 'breaching'.

A recovering species

Due to large-scale whaling in the 1940s and 1950s, the humpback whale population declined from around 25,000 to under 500. Whaling was banned in the early 1960s, and the humpback population is now estimated at over 33,000–35,000 worldwide.

Snubfin dolphin

Australian snubfin dolphins are vulnerable to human activity on the reef because they live close to the shore and so often get caught in fishing nets or can get struck by boats. As a result, their numbers are in decline.

Be smart, survive!

To be a good whale watcher, you need patience. Whales may be curious, but they're also cautious, and it may take up to an hour before they are confident enough to make a close approach. They prefer open spaces with plenty of depth, and that means you often end up dangling in the middle of a serious swell. Remember: never approach a whale; let it come to you.

Watching whales and dolphins

Because the Great Barrier Reef is an important breeding ground for whales and dolphins, strict measures are put in place to ensure tourists do not disturb them. For example, tourist vessels should never cross the path of these creatures. Tourists should not swim within 100 m of a whale or 50 m of a dolphin; nor should they attempt to touch or feed a cetacean.

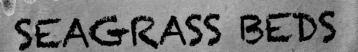

SEAGRASS BEDS

20 October

My southward journey along the Great Barrier Reef has taken me to Hinchinbrook Island, where I've spent time snorkelling in the seagrass beds. They are underwater grassy meadows that sway in the shallow waters. I was lucky enough to spot a herd of dugongs grazing and see why these gentle giants are known as 'sea cows'.

Hinchinbrook Island

Seagrass beds

Hinchinbrook Island

Undersea meadows

Seagrasses are flowering plants that grow under the sea. They got their name because many of the species have long, narrow leaves and look a lot like grass. They grow mainly in shallow, sheltered, coastal waters with sandy or muddy bottoms, where they form extensive 'meadows'. These are grazed by hundreds of species, including green turtles, dugongs, manatees, sea birds and sea urchins. They also provide a home for 134 species of fish, most of which feed not on the seagrass itself but on the tiny animals that eat it.

The dugong has paddle-like forelimbs which it uses to move around the seagrass beds.

Dugong and green turtle

Dugongs are distantly related to elephants. They grow to about 3 m in length, weigh up to 400 kg and can live for 70 years. Dugongs are the farmers of the seagrass beds. By intensively grazing their favourite varieties, they increase the nutrition value of the plant when it regrows. Another commonly sighted species here is the green turtle. As hatchlings, these turtles feed on small fish and crustaceans. But as adults they turn vegetarian and dine exclusively on seagrasses.

Snorkelling safety tips

- Always snorkel with a partner and stay in sight of each other.
- Stay close to shore or your boat. If you get tired, roll onto your back and tread water for a few minutes.
- To avoid exhaustion, use a flotation device such as a snorkelling vest.
- Be aware of the seabed. Avoid very shallow waters, where coral and other rough surfaces can cause injury.

GET OUT ALIVE !!

MANGROVES AND SALT MARSHES

28 October

Late October finds me in Bowling Green Bay, a national park of wetlands and mountainous rainforest. I'm here to explore the salt marshes and mangrove forests of its coastal plain, and to see if I can spot a saltwater crocodile. The encounter I'd been hoping for (and dreading!) happened on my third day. I was in a swampy area on the western side of the bay when I caught sight of a 'saltie' sunning itself. Its huge jaws hung open, but luckily it didn't seem too hungry. I took a few photos, then beat a hasty retreat!

Townsville and Bowling Green Bay

Townsville

Bowling Green Bay

Mangrove

Salt marsh

Valuable habitats

Mangroves are trees that grow in areas regularly flooded by tides, such as estuaries, rivers and bays. Salt marshes are usually found on the landward side of mangroves and are made up of salt-tolerant flowering plants. Mangroves and salt marshes cover around 3,800 km² of the Great Barrier Reef coastline and provide a habitat for both marine and land species, such as young fish, crustaceans and birds. They protect the coast from storms and filter pollutants from rivers that would otherwise end up on the reefs.

The saltwater crocodile is the largest reptile on the planet, and perhaps the most likely to eat a human. It's big and strong enough to drag large animals, including cows, horses and water buffalo into the water and kill them with a single bite to the skull. Salties are most commonly found in rivers, swamps and estuaries, both here in Australia and also in India and South–East Asia. They're brilliant swimmers and have been spotted far out to sea. They average 4–5 m in length, but there have been reports of monsters of up to 7 m!

Avoid being eaten by a crocodile

GET OUT ALIVE!!

- Never swim in water where crocodiles may live.
- When fishing, always stand a few metres back from the water's edge.
- Never clean fish or discard fish scraps near the water's edge.
- Never dangle your arms or legs over the side of a boat.
- Remember: crocodiles are more likely to attack at night and during the breeding season: September to April.

FLINDERS REEF

Flinders Reef

North Reef

Watanabe — Bommie

The Soft Spot

Lonely Eel

Anemone City

Rock Arch

Flinders Cay

North Boomerang Reef

China Wall

Sand Cay

Cod Wall

Scuba Zoo

South Boomerang Reef

6 November

After an enjoyable week on Bowling Green Bay, I set my course for Flinders Reef, 220 km to the east – said to be a great spot to observe sharks. I moored my boat at Watanabe Bommie. After entering the water, I was surrounded by a mass of silver mackerel and tuna. Suddenly, a grey reef shark appeared beneath me and plunged into the school of fish. I watched, mesmerised by the flashing movements of silver as the fish tried to evade the shark's jaws!

Sharks

The Great Barrier Reef and Coral Sea reefs are home to around 125 species of shark and rays. The most commonly sighted sharks are the black-tip and white-tip reef sharks. The more remote Coral Sea reefs, such as Osprey, Holmes and Flinders attract the grey reef, oceanic silvertip and hammerhead – tempted there by shoals of tuna, mackerel and barracuda.

Scientists believe that the hammerhead's T-shaped head helps it to hunt.

Coral paradise

Flinders Reef is a wonderful dive site, full of pinnacles, undersea cliffs and coral gardens. I did a wall dive (exploring an underwater cliff face) along Rock Arch, where I found giant coral heads interconnecting to form mini-caves, and a gorgonian (a soft coral that looks like a giant fan) that was 4 m across. Another site, Anemone City, has five pinnacles with tops covered in anemones. Swimming around their coral-covered walls are angelfish, fairy basslets and butterfly fish.

Be smart, survive!

While I was at Flinders Reef, I checked out the wreck of Australian army ship *Crusader*, which was sunk here in 1986. Wreck diving is fascinating, but dangerous. Remember:
- Wrecks are often fragile and break easily.
- Always take a cutting device in case you get entangled with a fishing line or rope.
- Take a spare light source in case your dive light fails.
- If you go inside a wreck, use a guideline to help you find your way out more easily.

Avoid a shark attack

Of the many hundreds of shark species, only about 20 are dangerous to humans. To avoid being attacked:

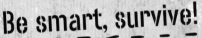

- Stay with other swimmers: a group can maintain a better look-out and can more easily fight off an aggressive shark.
- If you're on a boat, don't throw rubbish or fish scraps overboard, as it will attract sharks.
- If a shark approaches, keep still and it will usually swim away.
- If the shark attacks, kick and strike it. Hit it on the gills or in the eyes, if at all possible.

THE CORAL CAY

13 November

It's the start of the wet season, and the clouds are heavy with rain as I head south to Heron Island, a coral cay 72 km north-east of Gladstone. The island is just 800 m by 300 m, and in the swelling seas I nearly missed it. I'd heard the island is a major nesting site, but I was unprepared for the sheer numbers of birds there. When I arrived, I saw hundreds in every tree – dozens nesting on each branch. At night the mating calls are so loud, I have to wear earplugs.

Turtles

Heron Island is also an important nesting site for green turtles. Many have swum more than 2,600 km from their feeding ground to get here, often returning to the same beach from which they hatched. The female moves up the beach, digs a hole with her hind flippers and lays her eggs. Then she covers the nest of eggs with sand and returns to the sea. The eggs hatch 45–75 days later. The hatchlings head straight for the water, but many do not make it – eaten by predators such as gulls and crabs.

Eastern reef egret

Birds

Coral cays are small, low—lying sandy islands that develop on reefs due to waves or tidal currents lifting sediment to the surface. Heron Island provides a home for a variety of birds, including silver gulls, eastern reef egrets and buff—banded rails. During the breeding season (October to April), tens of thousands more seabirds arrive, including the wedge—tailed shearwaters and over 70,000 black or white—capped noddies.

Buff-banded rail

Be smart, survive!

Birds are vulnerable during nesting. Slight disturbances can scare an adult bird from the nest, leaving the eggs exposed to predators. Here are some bird-watching tips:
- Land and launch your boat well away from any birds.
- Stay away from nesting birds; crouch, keep quiet and move slowly.
- Never try to touch birds, chicks or eggs.
- Take care during late afternoons, early evenings, wet or cold weather, or moonlit nights when eggs and chicks are most vulnerable.
- Back away if the birds exhibit signs of stress, such as raucous calling, swooping or dive-bombing.

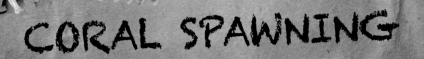

CORAL SPAWNING

17 November

Today I made for Lady Elliot Island at the southern end of the marine park, where I was lucky enough to witness a coral spawning. It was during a night dive. I suddenly found myself in a thick upside-down blizzard of white specks as the corals simultaneously released their eggs and sperm. I could feel the eggs like droplets on my skin as they floated up towards the surface. To clear away the 'fog' and see where I was going, I had to blow out in front of me from my breathing valve.

Annual event

On one night each year, for just two hours or so, more than 400 types of coral simultaneously release their eggs and sperm on the Great Barrier Reef, forming a slick on the surface of the sea that lasts for days. This is how the coral reproduces. A single mass spawning event like this is useful for coral because it means there's far too much spawn produced at one time for predators to eat. Also, it allows the corals to inter-breed, which helps them to evolve and become stronger.

Coral danger

Avoid touching coral: it is easily damaged and can cut through skin. Clean cuts thoroughly by scrubbing with a brush and flushing the affected area with saline solution.

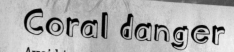

Unpredictable

Massed coral spawning was first scientifically observed in 1981. It takes place each year between October and December on the Great Barrier Reef, but predicting exactly when has proved impossible, because the coral gives no sign that the spawning is about to start until about half an hour beforehand. However, researchers have worked out that spawning always takes place at night about three to five days after the full moon, when the water is calm. The water temperature needs to be around 27°C.

Be smart, survive!

Night diving is fun. Your dive light will reveal a whole new cast of aquatic characters. But remember:
• Choose a dive site that you are familiar with.
• Start at twilight so that you can gradually get used to the darkness.
• Plan shorter, shallower dives. Typically scuba divers use more air on night dives, so a scuba tank will not last as long.
• Always carry a spare dive light.

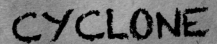

2 December

As I started to head back north towards Cairns, the weather got worse. The coastguard advised me that there was a tropical depression on my route, so I turned west. Bad move! The depression was also heading that way, and turning into a full-blown cyclone. For the next 36 hours, I was hit by driving rain, rough seas and wind gusting at 60 knots. I had no choice but to drop sails, stow all my gear below decks, batten down the hatches and retire to my bunk.

Townsville
Prosperine
Whitsunday Islands
Brampton Island
Macay
Rockhampton
Great Keppel Island
Gladstone
Heron Island

Spinning fury

A cyclone is a furious, whirling storm system that brings torrential rain, thunder, lightning and winds that can reach more than 250 km per hour. They occur in tropical parts of the world and are known as hurricanes in the Americas, and typhoons in South—East Asia. At sea, cyclones generate waves big enough to wreck ships, and on land they cause floods, smash buildings and hurl trees and cars into the air. In Australia, cyclone season runs from November until April.

This satellite image show Cyclone Yasi approaching the north-east coast of Australia in February 2011.

Reef destroyer

Cyclones cause extensive damage to the Great Barrier Reef. Between 1985 and 2012, the reef lost half of its coral; cyclone damage was responsible for 48% of this loss. Cyclones break up coral structures. Their heavy rains decrease salt levels, which kills many of the animals that inhabit the reef. They cause floods along the coasts, and when the floodwater, now polluted with agricultural chemicals, runs back into the sea, it further damages the reef.

Cyclone damage caused to the delicate coral beds.

Be smart, survive!

If you find yourself sailing into or near a cyclone, take the following safety measures:
• Tidy away or secure all loose objects on deck (unsecured objects can become dangerous missiles).
• Batten down all hatches.
• Close any watertight doors.
• Board up all panes of glass.
• Ensure a lifejacket and lifebuoy are close at hand.
• Report the position of your boat to the coastguard.
• Record the path of the storm and listen to weather bulletins.

Falling overboard

If you find yourself in the water and you need to be rescued, the most important thing is to relax. Your body's natural buoyancy will keep at least the top of your head, including your face, above water. Floating on your back takes the least energy. Lie on your back, spread your arms and legs and arch your back. That way your face will always be out of the water.

GET OUT ALIVE!!

23

CORAL BLEACHING

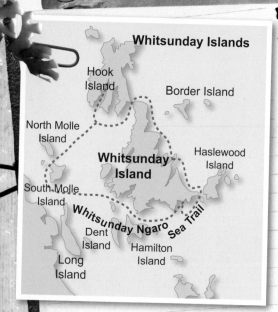

Whitsunday Islands

Hook Island

Border Island

North Molle Island

Whitsunday Island

Haslewood Island

South Molle Island

Whitsunday Ngaro Sea Trail

Dent Island

Hamilton Island

Long Island

7 January

It's now high summer. The days are hot and sunny, and I've arrived in the beautiful Whitsunday Islands, comprising 74 islands midway along the Queensland coast. I was diving in Blue Pearl Bay off Hook Island, and was saddened to see that the coral had lost its beautiful colours. Where I had expected to see vivid reds, pinks, greens and yellows, all was a ghostly white, like a dead forest.

Losing colour

Coral gets its colour from algae, called zooxanthellae, that live in the coral's tissue. The coral gets food from the algae and the algae get a safe place to live. But when water temperatures rise, the coral expels the algae and so turns white. This process is called coral bleaching. The coral is still alive, and if water temperatures fall, the algae will return. If not, the coral will starve and die. Due to global warming, sea temperatures have risen, and these bleaching events are more common. The worst mass bleaching on record was in 2002 when 55% of the reefs on the Great Barrier Reef suffered bleaching. About 5% of the coral reefs were severely damaged.

Avoid getting stung

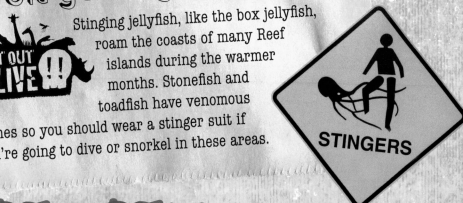

Stinging jellyfish, like the box jellyfish, roam the coasts of many Reef islands during the warmer months. Stonefish and toadfish have venomous spines so you should wear a stinger suit if you're going to dive or snorkel in these areas.

STINGERS

Crown of Thorns

Another threat to the reef is the Crown of Thorns starfish. This giant predator, which has up to 21 arms covered in poisonous spikes, can eat as much as 10 m² of living coral every year. The starfish eats by pushing its stomach out through its mouth, digesting an area equal to its own diameter in one swoop. It is thought to have been responsible for 42% of all coral death on the Great Barrier Reef between 1985 and 2012. When Crown of Thorns starfish numbers are low, corals can recover from any damage caused by their feeding. Starfish population booms usually occur about once every 80 years, but they are now happening more frequently. Scientists think it is due to nutrients, pesticides and other pollutants from farms entering waters around the Reef and helping more of the starfish larvae to survive.

THE TRADITIONAL OWNERS

13 January

I've just done the Whitsunday Ngaro Sea Trail. It was an enjoyable combination of kayaking and picturesque walks on and around Whitsunday, South Molle and Hook Islands. The terrain included forests, grasslands, sandy beaches and rugged peaks, and some of the views from the mountaintops took my breath away. I also learned about the Ngaro people, who have lived on the Whitsundays for over 9,000 years. On the walk, I passed a cave containing ancient Ngaro rock art.

Whitehaven beach on Whitsunday Island.

Map labels:
Whitsunday Islands
Hook Island
Border Island
North Molle Island
Haslewood Island
Whitsunday Island
South Molle Island
Whitsunday Ngaro Sea Trail
Dent Island
Hamilton Island
Long Island

Aboriginal people

The first Australians were the Aboriginal people. They have been living on this continent for around 40,000 years. Aboriginal groups, such as the Ngaro, Umpila and Lama Lama, who live on the Queensland coast, have had a long association with the Great Barrier Reef. For thousands of years they have fished here, using wooden canoes and spears. They have left evidence of this in paintings, sorcery sites and other archaeological remains. Today, the Aboriginal people continue to fish, but with more modern equipment. They have kept alive their culture through storytelling, music and art.

Torres Strait Islander people

The other indigenous people of the Great Barrier Reef are the Torres Strait Islanders. They are a seafaring people related to the Melanesians of the south–west Pacific. Their homeland is the Torres Strait, in northern Australia, where the Great Barrier Reef begins. The Torres Strait Islanders have always fished, hunting reef animals such as dugongs and sea turtles. On the outer islands of the Great Barrier Reef they collect bird and turtle eggs, bird droppings (used as fertiliser) and feathers. They have built up trade networks with the natives of Papua New Guinea, trading turtle shell and pearl shell for drums, snakeskins and bamboo spears.

The Torres Strait Islanders have traditionally dived for pearls and other shells, to make products that they can trade.

Dangers in the shallows

GET OUT ALIVE!!

The bays and estuaries of these islands are beautiful, but can harbour hidden dangers. Stepping on a sea urchin, for example, can produce pain and infection, and the spines are often very difficult to remove. When moving about in shallow water, always wear some form of footwear and try not to pick up your feet as you walk – it's better to shuffle them along the bottom.

Sea urchins live in shallow seas where they feed on algae.

THE END OF THE TRIP

3 February

This morning, as I sailed back into Cairns Seaport, I admit my eyes were a little damp, and it wasn't just from the sea spray. It's the end of the trip! I've had such an amazing time over the past five months. There were so many highlights – swimming with whales, exploring coral gardens, kayaking around the Whitsundays – I can't begin to decide which I enjoyed the most. The strong feeling I'm left with is that the Great Barrier Reef is a rare and beautiful jewel in our natural world, and we must do everything we can to protect it.

World Wildlife Fund

Organisations such as the World Wildlife Fund for Nature (WWF) are working with the Australian fishing industry to try to safeguard the Great Barrier Reef from overfishing. They are providing scientific advice on harvest limits, and pushing for a ban on fishing gear that results in the by-catch of sea birds, turtles, whales, dolphins and threatened fish species.

Sustainable fishing

One major threat to the Great Barrier Reef comes from overfishing. When fishing vessels target particular species, it can upset the reef's ecological balance. For example, overfishing of grouper fish has led to a rise in the numbers of damselfish (the grouper's main prey). Damselfish create pockets in corals where the algae they feed upon can grow. But too many pockets can cause the algae to take over a reef, eventually killing it.

Be smart, survive!

If we care about the survival of the Great Barrier Reef, then we should visit as eco-tourists. We should interact with the local people, respect the local environment and take photos, but not collect corals or shells as souvenirs!

Sustainable farming

The Great Barrier Reef is also threatened by pollution from agriculture. When it rains, fertilizers and pesticides in the fields are washed into waterways and eventually end up in the sea and on the reef. Conservationist groups launched Project Catalyst in 2008, which advises farmers on how to reduce the amount of fertilizers and pesticides they use. This has already resulted in an improvement in water quality on the Great Barrier Reef.

This scientist is studying the effects of ocean acidification around the Great Barrier Reef.

GLOSSARY

aft At, near or towards the back end of a boat.

algae A group of simple, non-flowering plants that includes seaweeds and many single-celled organisms.

Antarctica The continent around the South Pole.

bommie The local name for a column of coral reef that rises up out of the surrounding reef and is often exposed at low tide.

buoyancy The ability to float in water.

by-catch The unwanted fish or other marine creatures caught during commercial fishing for a different species.

conservationist A person or organisation that campaigns or acts for the protection of the natural environment.

crustaceans A family of creatures that includes crabs, lobsters, shrimps and barnacles.

cumulus cloud A fairly low-altitude cloud formed of rounded masses heaped on each other above a flat base.

dinghy A small, open boat, usually with a mast and sails, used for racing or recreation.

dive computer A small computer worn on the wrist that monitors depth throughout the dive and tells divers when they should return to the surface. It also tells them if they need to take a safety stop before reaching the surface to avoid any risk of 'the bends'.

dive light A torch used by divers.

ecotourism Tourism that aims to support conservation efforts in threatened natural environments.

estuary The tidal area near the mouth of a river, where the tide meets the river flow.

evolve Develop gradually from a simple to a more complex form.

fish nursery A natural habitat where young fish are bred and nurtured.

fore At, near or towards the front of a boat.

global warming The gradual increase in the overall temperature of the Earth's atmosphere, which is partly caused by human activities.

hatchling A young animal that has recently emerged from its egg.

imprint Impression or mark.

indigenous Native to an area.

kayak A type of canoe made of a light frame with a watertight covering and a small opening at the top to sit in.

lagoon A stretch of salt water separated from the sea by a low sandbank or coral reef.

marine Of or found in the sea.

outrigger canoe A canoe that has a beam projecting from its side in order to stabilise it.

polyp A creature with a column-shaped body, topped by a mouth surrounded by a ring of tentacles. Polyps include the animals that create coral reefs.

rainforest A dense forest, rich in plant and animal life, with consistently heavy rainfall, usually found in tropical areas.

saline solution A saltwater solution used to clean wounds.

scuba A portable breathing apparatus for divers, consisting of cylinders of compressed air strapped on the diver's back, feeding air automatically through a mouthpiece. Scuba stands for self-contained underwater breathing apparatus.

sediment Matter that is carried by water or wind and deposited on the surface of the land and may in time form into rock.

snorkel A tube curving upwards from the mouth, allowing a diver to breathe while his or her head is in the water.

snorkelling vest An inflatable item that is worn around the neck like a bib and aids buoyancy for snorkellers.

spawn The eggs of coral polyps or other creatures, usually released in large numbers.

stinger suit A thick, waterproof suit that protects divers against stinging sea creatures.

sustainable Carried out in a way that minimises damage to the environment.

swell A slow, regular movement of the sea in rolling waves that do not break.

tarpaulin Heavy-duty waterproof cloth.

tropical depression A circling system of clouds and thunderstorms that lacks the organisation or spiral shape of more powerful storms. Tropical depressions can turn into cyclones.

venom Poisonous fluid secreted by animals.

weightbelt A heavy belt worn by divers to counteract the buoyancy of other diving equipment.

wetland An area of marshes and swamps where the land is permanently or seasonally saturated with water.

INDEX & FURTHER INFORMATION

Books

Great Barrier Reef (Big Outdoors) by V Bodden (Creative Education, 2010)

The Great Barrier Reef (Nature's Wonders) by P Kummer (Marshall Cavendish, 2008)

Great Barrier Reef (Troubled Treasures) by C Kennedy (Checkerboard Books, 2011)

Inside a Coral Reef (Amazing Journeys) by C Telford and R Theodorou (Heinemann, 2006)

Websites

http://ngm.nationalgeographic.com/2011/05/great-barrier-reef/holland-text

http://www.bbc.co.uk/nature/places/Great_Barrier_Reef

http://adventure.howstuffworks.com/great-barrier-reef.htm

http://www.telegraph.co.uk/travel/destinations/australiaandpacific/australia/737868/Exploring-the-Great-Barrier-Reef.html